The Bishopric

*A Handbook on
Creating Episcopacy in the
African-American
Pentecostal Church*

By

BISHOP J. DELANO ELLIS, II

© Copyright 2003 J. Delano Ellis II. All rights reserved.

No part of this publication may be reproduced, stored in a retrieval system, or transmitted, in any form or by any means, electronic, mechanical, photocopying, recording, or otherwise, without the written prior permission of the author.

All Scripture quotations are taken from the Authorized Ki ng James Version of the Bible unless otherwise noted.

The Bishopric:
A Handbook on Creating Episcopacy in the African-American Pentecostal Church

10515 Chester Avenue, Cleveland, OH 44106
Phone: (216) 721-5934 Fax: (216) 721-6938

```
National Library of Canada Cataloguing in Publication Data

Ellis, J. Delano (Jesse Delano)
      The bishopric : a handbook on creating episcopacy in
the African-American Penticostal church / J. Delano Ellis
II.
Includes bibliographical references.
ISBN 1-55395-848-9
      1. African American Pentecostal churches.  2. Episco-
pacy.
I. Title.
BX8762.5.Z5E45 2003    289.9'4'08996073          C2003-
901019-8
```

TRAFFORD

This book was published *on-demand* in cooperation with Trafford Publishing.
On-demand publishing is a unique process and service of making a book available for retail sale to the public taking advantage of on-demand manufacturing and Internet marketing. **On-demand publishing** includes promotions, retail sales, manufacturing, order fulfilment, accounting and collecting royalties on behalf of the author.

Suite 6E, 2333 Government St., Victoria, B.C. V8T 4P4, CANADA
Phone   250-383-6864   Toll-free   1-888-232-4444 (Canada & US)
Fax   250-383-6804   E-mail   sales@trafford.com
Web site www.trafford.com   TRAFFORD PUBLISHING IS A DIVISION OF TRAFFORD HOLDINGS LTD.
Trafford Catalogue #03-0211   www.trafford.com/robots/03-0211.html

10   9   8   7   6   5   4   3   2   1

TABLE OF CONTENTS

Foreword..vi

Acknowledgements..x

Dedication..xii

Introduction..xiii

Chapter I
"IN THE BEGINNING" THERE WAS A NEED......................................17

Chapter II
SUCCEEDING TO THE OFFICE...19

Chapter III
APOSTOLIC SUCCESSION 22

Chapter IV
EPISCOPAL ORDERS 24

Chapter V
EPISCOPAL GRACES 33

Chapter VI
RELATIONSHIPS WITH OTHER RELIGIOUS BODIES........................41

Chapter VII
LEVITICAL VESTMENTS and CODE OF DRESS 45

Chapter VIII
CELEBRATION VESTMENTS 57

Chapter IX
CIVIC WEAR (Bishops)...59

Chapter X
THE COLLEGE OF BISHOPS (Colors) 61

Chapter XI
OVERSEERS...63

Chapter XII
CIVIC WEAR (Overseers) 65

TABLE OF CONTENTS

Chapter XIII
ORDAINED AND NON-ORDAINED CLERGY 66

Chapter XIV
DEACONS 68

Chapter XV
EPILOGUE 70

Appendix
DOCUMENT ON HISTORICAL APOSTOLIC SUCCESSION 77

Bibliography 97

FOREWORD

Those of us blessed to experience professional vocations know the benefits of having guidelines or parameters in which to operate. The same holds true for the ministry. Likewise, we Pentecostals in the vocation of Pastoral and Episcopal ministry also know the frustrations of functioning in liturgical duties with no appropriate guides to assist us. Often when forced to seek assistance through materials from other mainline Denominations, we often experience difficulty by trying to superimpose their patterns on to our tradition. Fortunately for us, there is one among us who has blazed a trail as a result of his ministerial exposure to not only bring tools we can use, but a means by which some of the gaps between the religious streams can be bridged.

Many have watched him in awe from afar, while others have merely mimicked what they observed. Better still, others have been fortunate enough to be directly exposed to the genius of Bishop Jesse Delano Ellis, II, a churchman, indeed. Like thousands of others, I first encountered the genius of his keen sense of worship and respect for liturgical order while attending the Holy Convocation of the Church of God in Christ for the first time. Always believing that Pentecostals could have order with our ardor, I saw the abstract become concrete reality. Moreover, through the tutelage of this man, I was able to bring to the bishops and the Bible Way World Wide organization this succession of liturgical order within Apostolic Pentecostalism. Soon, one man's vision for his denomination became the catalyst by which all of Pentecost could be exposed to a new appreciation for Early Church liturgics. As his center of gravity began to shift from his early exposure to the Episcopal church, his pioneer years in the Church of God in Christ as liturgist and the conceptual founder of the Adjutancy, Bishop Ellis was being prepared to influence Pentecostalism in a paradigm shift with regard to the Bishopric. Like it or not, credited or not, Bishop Ellis and his 'high church' thrust has affected the Pentecostals and Charismatics at large. Moreover, as the father of the Adjutancy, he mentored those of us who would be churchmen, to appreciate the Office of Bishop and our Levitical priestly role as servants of the Lord's house.

The fact remains that the Church of Jesus Christ our Lord is universally one, holy and apostolic, and all that has truly affected its development has had a relationally unifying element. Just as the Church is built upon the apostles and prophets, so it is with every major shift or move towards the maturing of the Church. Everything is a successive link. To this end, in March 1984, history was made in many of our African-American Pentecostal denominations, when Bishop J.O. Patterson, Sr., Presiding Bishop of the Church of God in Christ, called a delegation of denominational leaders to Memphis, Tennessee, (the 'Jerusalem' of the Church of God in Christ.) Bishop Patterson was elected to serve the World Fellowship of the Black Pentecostal Churches as its founding President. As a principal organizer of the World Fellowship of Black Pentecostal Churches, Bishop Ellis served as the Executive Secretary, further distinguishing himself as an ecumenist and a proponent for unity among African-American Pentecostals and their world renown.

Later, as a Bishop and the Presiding Prelate of the United Pentecostal Churches of Christ, Bishop Ellis took the vision of his spiritual father, Bishop J.O. Patterson, as the impetus to organize the Joint College of African-American Pentecostal Bishops - with Bishops Roy E. Brown, Presiding Bishop of Pilgrim Assemblies, Paul S. Morton, Presiding Bishop of the Full Gospel Baptist Church Fellowship, and Wilbert S. McKinley, the Metropolitan of the College, all sharing as its co-founders. These were the seeds for the African-American *classical* Pentecostal movement's becoming of age. As a Joint College, it was also a recognition of the apostolicity that exists among themselves - whether mega or micro, Oneness or Trinitarians, male or female. Historically, as

African-American Pentecostals, we have ascribed to an Episcopal form of government for our denominations and organizational groups. With the Joint College of African-American Pentecostal Bishops' Congress as the conduit, Bishop Ellis is making available (to a wider audience), his years of experience and knowledge of the Episcopal ministry, while edifying this august body of bishops.

Consequently, as we now approach the one-hundredth anniversary of the Azusa Street Revival, we have, through this new text, a milestone of how far we have come. Through this book, Bishop Ellis has made available much of what makes us one in communion with the '*ancient pilgrim*' Church, while remaining uniquely Pentecostal in faith and tradition. I enjoyed reading the manuscript. I even more enjoyed reflecting upon our generation's participation in this paradigm shift that will provide for future generations, tools for excellence as the Lord delays His coming. Finally, for those of us who have been praying for Bishop Ellis to write, we trust this book and subject is an installment for more books to come.

Bishop Carl H. Montgomery, II, D. Min.
Presiding Prelate,
Harvest Time Covenant Fellowship and
Senior Pastor, Greater Grace Harvest Church
Headquarters - Baltimore, Maryland

ACKNOWLEDGEMENTS

I take this moment to express my deepest thanks and appreciation to the many who continue to encourage me to put in writing those things which the Fathers put in me. I would suppose that every preacher and student of the Word of God writes volumes within a lifetime, as have I, but to sit down and prepare a work for generations to read feels like an impossible task.

Were it not for people like Bishop Alfred A. Owens, Bishop Carl H. Montgomery, II, Bishop Luther James Blackwell, Bishop Eric Daniel Garnes, Bishop James Ronald Chambers, Bishop Benjamin Terwood Douglass, Bishop Larry Darnell Trotter, Bishop T. Lane Grant, Overseer Marian Denise Hickman, Elder Yvonne Tufts-Jeans (*who purchased and gave me my first personal tape recorder for this purpose*), Elder W. Michelle James-Moore, Minister Sheila Ann Webb, Overseer Gwendolyn Gilbert-Saunders, Deacon David Delano Cottingham, Elder Allen Farrow (*who serves as my Adjutant-Apostolic and who salvaged and organized my manuscripts*), Elder Lillian Marion Ellis, Overseer Darryl Dion Woodson, Dr. Johnny W. Wade, Sister Minette Jackson (*who proofread this manuscript, made sure the book was designed and printed*), and my mother-in-law, Mother Almyra Henderson-

Battles (*who also proofread this particular manuscript*) and countless others, this particular volume would not have been prepared. To the Members of Pentecostal Church of Christ in Cleveland, Ohio, I appreciate your encouragement most of all.

I take this means to thank God for and to honor my daughter in the Ministry, Minister Lynece (Necie) Dawson, whose weekly nagging has come to fruition. Necie is asleep in Jesus, but her constant encouragement and weekly inquiries cause me to name her among my heroes. More than all of the foregoing, my wife and daughter in the Ministry, Overseer Sabrina Joyce Ellis, is the one driving force behind this and any other book that we've made available to you. I owe *Sabrina* a debt of gratitude that I will never be able to repay.

To the many sons and daughters to whom I have transferred the blessedness of Ordained and Consecrated Succession, I offer this one Benediction: "*Be thou faithful unto death; and He will give you a crown of life.*"

+ J. DELANO ELLIS, II
January 2003, A.D.

DEDICATION

This work is dedicated to the Memory of my sainted grandmother, and mother, Dr. Martha Ann Ellis, and Mother Lucy Mae Ellis who loved me and prayed for me. *"They rest from their labors."*

My greatest tribute is given to my Partner in the Gospel Ministry, Faithful Student, Pastor, Wife, and Greatest Fan,

"SABRINA"

INTRODUCTION

When this College was ordered by the Lord and it was made clear that Episcopal-styled training was to become the curriculum by which we would be governed, the Co-Founders trusted the Lord to give us a person who would mentor us and bring honor to the Name of Jesus Christ and particular Glory to His Church in our times. It became needful for us to adopt a Code of Dress and habit that would set us apart from congregationalism. We found the need to re-think the theology of the Pentecostal fathers and forge a witness that included the entire Baptized Body of Jesus Christ everywhere.

Our message had to be clear and unadulterated by the modernists. Our theology had to be cleansed of the separatist preaching which, for more than a century, kept Christians estranged from each other.

It was then time to create a College for the Princes of the Church, *"So that we might all walk by the same rule and mind the same thing."* Our fellowships of Congregations need an example and our Bishops are called upon to be the example-fathers of the New Millennium, in all things.

In several places throughout this book, you may discover where the terms "we" or "us" are used when the intent is to speak of ourselves in the first person singular. To some this may be confusing, but this brief note is to explain that bishops never use the personal pronoun, "I" when referring to themselves. Neither does a bishop use the word, "my" when expressing possession.

In Royal Courts, Sovereigns never refer to themselves in the first person singular because they speak in the majesty of their office as Potentates for a Government. Their reference is not in the plural, but rather to speak of the immensity of their office. God spoke in creation and said, *"Let Us make man. . ."* When He did this He was not talking about a committee but rather He was speaking in the immensity of His office and power as Creator and Maker of all things. God's very Name is in the plural sense because He fills all in all, and all things are in Him.

Bishops should learn to use the plural sense, especially in writing Missives and Epistles to Believers in Christ because we speak, not for ourselves, but for Christ and His Kingdom. When a bishop says "we," that bishop is referring to Christ, first and foremost, and then him/herself.

In closing, it might also be helpful to remember that we should never sign our names using the title "Bishop" in front of it. But rather, we should use the simple marking of the sign of the Cross and then our given and surname: (+ John Harrison Doe)

Our secretaries should be told to type our titles in the letter (Bishop John Harrison Doe) but we must sign above the typewritten text as described herein. That Cross is our acknowledgement of "Christ" Who causes us to triumph. It also says, *"We sign this document in Christ's stead."*

Now, herein lays a Constitution and Code of Canons, which will govern the Church fathers, and our sons and daughters who will follow us in African-American Pentecostalism.

Chapter I

"IN THE BEGINNING" -- THE NEED

One late afternoon in the Summer of 1994, four men were traveling from New York to Philadelphia for the purpose of purchasing vestments and insignia for the Episcopal Office. While traveling, Archbishop Wilbert Sterling McKinley and Archbishop Roy Edmund Brown, both of Brooklyn, New York, along with Bishop J. Delano Ellis, of Cleveland, Ohio were discussing the need for providing assistance and training for the proliferated Episcopacy within the African-American Pentecostal Community. After lengthy discussion, a telephone call was made to Bishop Paul Sylvester Morton of New Orleans, Louisiana. Bishop Morton expressed his desire to join with these men in forming this College and Bishop Ellis was elected to preside over this venture.

The name chosen for the organization

The Bishopric

was: "THE JOINT COLLEGE OF AFRICAN-AMERICAN PENTECOSTAL BISHOPS," aka "THE JOINT COLLEGE OF BISHOPS," and the Headquarters was ordered to be situated in the Seat of the Founding Presidency:

The Joint College of Bishops
10515 Chester Avenue
Cleveland, Ohio 44106
(United States of America)

Chapter II

SUCCEEDING TO THE OFFICE

All bishops of this College are appointed by the Presiding Bishop of their respective Churches or elected by their deliberate Body of Presbyters, who alone, have the constitutional authority to do so. The process is reasonably difficult, but that, in itself, assures the Church of legitimate episcopates with the highest caliber of credentia.

When a person has been appointed/elected to the Bishopric, their Presiding Bishop assigns the chief adjutant and the chairman of the Denomination's Episcopal Committee to begin the preparation and final investigations into the validity of the designate's License, Ordination, and ministry. After copies of Licenses and all Ordinations have been received by the Presiding Bishop's Office, a formal Letter of Request must be signed by the

The Bishopric

designate and sent to the Presiding Bishop requesting Ordination and Consecration to the Office for which they have been selected or elected.

In those rare cases when a group of ordained pastors have themselves elected one of their number to serve as their leader, the President Bishop of the Joint College may receive a Letter of Request from the bishop-elect, requesting his services as Chief Consecrator and Convener of a College of Bishops for investigation and subsequent Ordination to the Office. After receiving the foregoing, the Episcopal Committee and the chief adjutant should then proceed to contact the principal clergy of the diocese for which the new bishop will be consecrated. The diocese must then send a Letter of Commendation, *signed by the clergy or their representative committee*, for their new bishop. The letter should also request consecration for the same. Since a bishop must have *"a good report from within and without"* it is necessary for us to know of the Candidate's work and life in the business and social community of the area where they serve. Therefore, Letters of Recommendation are welcomed for the Candidate's portfolio.

Chapter III

APOSTOLIC SUCCESSION

No person should have the right to exercise or conduct themselves in any of the Episcopal Matters of our Churches without Apostolic Succession, and Episcopal Dispensation to do so. We believe that bishops are the direct descendants of the Lord Jesus Christ, through His Apostles. Because of that contention, we hold dear and inviolate our Apostolic Succession which we claim through Augustine of Rome, who was sent by the 'Holy See' to England to establish the English Church. Aside from Succession through the Western Stream, this College also holds this same Succession through the Syrian Orthodox Stream. *[Please refer to the Historical Documents on Apostolic Succession in the APPENDIX of this Book.]*

Apostolic Succession

The foregoing statement is not to suggest that we do not recognize any other God-appointed leaders and episcopates of other Christian Reformations and Communions. We only intend to contend for our own heritage within the ancient pilgrim Church family. We believe that Apostolic Succession avails nothing pertinent to eternal salvation. The only agent of life for the Church is the Holy Spirit. Bishops must be filled with the Holy Spirit according to *Acts 2:4* if the Church is to do the work of her Lord.

Chapter IV

EPISCOPAL ORDERS

There are six (6) Orders of the Prelature in the Church of Jesus Christ. Five of the Orders are Episcopal and one is Potentiary. For our purposes here, we will name the Orders of Prelature and then offer brief explanations according to their purviews. This list is not designed to subjugate anyone in either of the said Offices, but to provide a sense of "First Among Equals" that has always been the hallmark of the Apostolic Office.

(1) The Presiding Bishop
(Primate or General Overseer)

(2) The Ordinary
(Diocesan)

(3) The Coadjutor

(4) The Suffragan

Episcopal Orders

(5) The Auxiliary

(6) The Overseer

The <u>first</u> and, *probably,* the most celebrated Order in the Church is that of the <u>Presiding Bishop</u>. This is the *Primate* among his/her fellow-bishops who may hold the distinction of *General Overseer* for the Communion of Saints. This office is obtained through Apostolic Election. The Presiding Bishop is elected from among the existing bishops of the Reformation, who are the College or Board of Bishops. The election is a very confidential matter and is held by the Bishops in a "Closed-Door Session" called by the Secretary of the Board. When a vacancy occurs in this office, the Secretary of the Board calls for a 'Conclave' to be held within thirty days at the Headquarters of that Denomination or Fellowship. After much prayer, a secret ballot should be the means whereby the Presiding Bishop is elected. When that election has ended, each bishop is called upon to obey, and prayerfully support their newly elected *Primate*, and to encourage all others within their See to do the same.

The Presiding Bishop is the Chief Executive Officer of the corporation and General Overseer for the religious affairs of the Reformation. It is usually the responsibility of the Presiding Bishop to have oversight for the General Assembly, as *Chair*, and its annual conclave. He/she also serves as the President of the College of Bishops for their respective Reformation.

The Presiding Bishop should be the only power of appointment for any of the Prelatures of the Church. This provision may not apply in Reformations where a Board of Bishops makes this selection. District Overseers

Episcopal Orders

(Superintendents, Presiding Elders) may be recommended and even selected by the bishops in the several Sees *(Dioceses)*; however, it is the Presiding Bishop who must elevate them to the *domestic* rank of prelate in the Church.

The Presiding Bishop is always the Chief Consecrator and Ordainer for all persons selected for Episcopacy in any Church. When it is determined that the Presiding Bishop will conduct such Consecration, there must be, at least, two other bishops in attendance as Co-Consecrators with him/her. No bishop shall participate who has not been properly ordained by three bishops and who, themselves, do not have Apostolic Succession. In the event that the Presiding Bishop cannot fill the request for a Consecration, the Presiding Bishop may give the assignment to another *senior* bishop of the Church.

The <u>second</u> Order of the Bishopric is that

The Bishopric

of the <u>Diocesan</u> or *Ordinary*. This bishop has oversight of an Apostolic Province or Diocese. All congregations and institutions are assigned to an Ordinary for oversight.

Ordinations to the Priesthood *(eldership)* and the Diaconate *(deacons)* are within the purview of this office.

(1) Bishops (<u>only</u>) ordain deacons; *because deacons are the property of the bishop, on assignment to the local churches.*

(2) Bishops, assisted by members of the Presbytery (ordained elders), ordain elders; *because elders become the property of the whole Church and are collegial priests with their fellows.*

(3) Three bishops must be present to ordain and consecrate another bishop.

Celebration of the Blessed Sacraments, Dedication of the Churches and Institutions, Blessing of Babies, Weddings and any other

Episcopal Orders

functions that are peculiar to this Office shall be governed thereby, without need for approval from superiors or subordinates. The power of appointment is within the purview of this Order, within the See of his/her appointment, with the exception of prelates.

Judgments or Disciplinary Hearings are conducted by this bishop in accordance with your Church Canons and the Constitution of this College.

The educational and social welfare of the people of a diocese are the responsibility of the bishop having jurisdiction. The bishop shall exercise vision and give example by his/her own vital and godly piety in those things that make for a good witness in Christ.

The bishop is the Chief Defender of the Faith in his/her diocese. This officer stands against all heresy and idolatry with the one and only infallible Word of God. As *Defender of the*

Faith, the bishop is 'chief preacher' in congregate assemblies. The bishop shall be the expounder of the Magesterium *(teaching of the Faith and Doctrines)* of the Church. Without Magesterium the Church becomes a social club like any other. It is the bishop who encourages the ministers and deacons to *"study...."*

The <u>third</u> Order of Prelature is that of the <u>Coadjutor Bishop</u>. This prelate is consecrated to serve as chief assistant to an Ordinary, with immediate right to succession. This bishop is limited in authority within a diocese so long as the Ordinary presides. The Coadjutor serves as the executor of the Ordinary's directives.

The <u>fourth</u> Order is that of the <u>Suffragan Bishop</u>. This bishop is a cabinet prelate of the Presiding Bishop's office or of a diocesan, without right of succession. The principle role of this prelate is administrative. When deemed feasible, the Presiding Bishop may assign the

Episcopal Orders

Auxiliary to serve a diocese as *Interim* Ordinary when the Ordinary is unable to function.

The <u>fifth</u> Order of the Prelature is that of the <u>Auxiliary Bishop</u>. This prelate is usually *'national'* in responsibility. One who holds this Office is usually an administrative officer of the National Church, without diocesan portfolio or assignment. The Presiding Bishop appoints this officer to the Episcopacy and after consecration, the Presiding Bishop appoints this bishop to the particular board or "congregation of responsibility."

The <u>sixth</u> Order is that of the <u>Overseer</u>. This prelate serves as the right arm of the bishop in the diocese. These ordinariates assist in managing the districts of the dioceses and assist pastors in the growth and greater development of their parishes. Overseers have no authority in and of themselves, but by reason of their Apostolic Appointment they serve as executive board members of the diocese in which they are assigned.

All Overseers comprise the Board of Overseers of their Churches. This Board is the "Lower House" of prelates, and with the College of Bishops, this Board serves as members of the Joint Board of Directors for the denomination. An Overseer may assist bishops in the ordination of Elders ONLY and shall always assist the bishops in the Celebrations of our Redemption.

Chapter V

EPISCOPAL GRACES

In those instances when another Reformation requests the assistance or approval of your Church in creating *episcopacy*, it shall be the habit and responsibility of bishops to consult with their Presiding Bishop prior to committing one's self to that specific task. Denominational leaders should be encouraged to establish communion and contact with your Church through your Chief Prelate before you receive or partake of their Sacraments. Although these articles might appear *exclusive*, they are not intended to insult any segment of the Body of Christ but to protect the integrity and legitimacy of this Church as a conservative Communion in Holiness. *"Worship is not worship; until it is done 'in Spirit and in truth'."* If a Fellowship's worship is not clear and clearly Bibline and if one's theology is not historically and biblically correct, we must be very careful how we sanction their entry into holy places and offices of the ancient pilgrim Church.

No subordinate bishop of any Church shall be authorized to participate in the consecration or ordination of any religious community without prior written "<u>Dispensation</u>" from the Presiding Bishop of their Church.

Amidst the many graces of this office is the deference of the faithful and the community. There may be those times when you are dressed in the "Tonsorils" (*civic attire)* of your office and in a public or private place, and one seeks to greet you with the time-honored salutation of touching their lips (*kissing*) to your ring. When this happens please remember to be graceful and not majestic. Receive their homage with humility, remembering that it is

Episcopal Graces

Christ they honor and not you particularly. Just a kind word and a passing assurance of God's favor are all the people need for that day. Give it to them freely and gracefully.

It is recommended that each Prelate of this College read *"Ministerial Ethics and Etiquette"* by *(Bishop) Nolan B. Harmon.* This text is as relevant as any other in giving ministers a sense of *manners* as we exercise our office in the Lord's Church in this world community. It is required that we respect all men and women of religion and reverence them in their respective offices. In those instances where we come in contact with other Christian ministers, bishops, superintendents, overseers, presiding elders, presidents, etc., it is incumbent on us to be examples in genuine courtesy and veneration of their particular offices. In the case of non-Christian organizations, we would require that each of

The Bishopric

our bishops and/or prelates remember that there is never any justification for disrespecting any person. We pray that our leaders will show, by example, the greatest respect for those who do not agree with our theology and teach our subordinate ministers and parishioners to do the same.

No Bishop of our College shall have the right to enter another diocese to serve without prior knowledge of the bishop having jurisdiction. It might be well received if the *invited* bishop would write a note of *advisement* to the bishop of the area, advising of his/her invitation and intended visit. The bishop of the area should respond in kind. It is important for all prelates of this College to remember that we are ONE Church, ONE people, *celebrating* ONE Name. Our unity is far more valuable to us than opportunity. It is the intention of the Joint College Office to keep the bishops mindful of

Episcopal Graces

their collegiality, one with another, under all circumstances.

It shall be the tradition of this College to venerate the Office of Presiding Bishop in all of the Churches. The focal-point of authority in your reformation is the one whom the Lord has appointed and whom you elect to serve as *Primate* and Chief Pastor.

The Presiding Bishop is elected by the College of Bishops of his Church to serve a term of years as determined by the Church's Constitution. He becomes the *"Father-in-God"* for the bishops, prelates, pastors and elders of the Church. As Presiding Bishop, he is responsible for the growth, training, impartation of spiritual gifts, and the temporal welfare of the whole Church as well. The Presiding Bishop appoints all bishops, overseers, and all national departmental heads for the reformation.

The Bishopric

As *General Overseer* for the Church, he/she presides over the College of Bishops and the Joint Board of Prelates. This is referred to as the "Apostolic Division" of the Reformation. This division is the policy-making Board of the Church and governing Board for the Denomination.

As *President* he/she might preside over the law-making and doctrine-expressing Body of the Church, known as the General Assembly or the Legislative Congress. This body meets at such times as prescribed by the By-laws of the Church and is comprised of all prelates along with the elected clerical and lay delegates as required by Constitution.

The Presiding Bishop's presence demands excellence and respect from all and it is required that both bishops and overseers give and teach deference for this Holy Apostolic Office. The Episcopal Norms of Protocol must

Episcopal Graces

be observed and no bishop of the Church should usurp the office of Presiding Bishop, either by pretension in dress or by surreptitious behavior in administration. To do so shall be deemed a gross violation of manners and discipline. He/she is your spiritual Patriarch or Matriarch and all should observe to entreat him/her as such at all times.

The one thing that certainly must distinguish those who lead the Lord's Church is our relationship and fellowship with God Almighty through our Lord Jesus Christ. Sufficeth to say every leader in the Lord's Church must be filled with the Holy Ghost. Daily lifestyle, which represents Christ, must be the hallmark of the Church. Each leader is called upon to practice the life of Christ daily and to *"be...an example to the believers in all things."* Our vital and godly piety will speak volumes for our witness in Christ.

Prelates who are married are required to be in harmony with their spouses and to have their own children under subjection. Our example in loving our spouse and then our children qualifies us to manage the Church of God...*and in that order!*

It is vital that we maintain a daily talking relationship with the Lord. Our sense of consecration must be unbroken if we are to represent God to our communities. Bishops and overseers are the example to the pastors of the districts. By our examples, our pastors become imitators of us and subsequently, the pastors become examples *"to the flock over the which the Holy Ghost has made them overseers."*

Chapter VI

RELATIONSHIPS WITH OTHER RELIGIOUS BODIES

The Joint College of Bishops is *Anglican-Apostolic* by tradition. Our roots reach back to Jesus Christ and His Apostles, which He chose, and through their successors, the patriarchs, and bishops of the Church, until this very present time. The Church is multi-faceted. We are not the only saints! Whenever the Church seeks to be alone and estranged from the rest of the *pilgrim* Church, that Fellowship runs the risk of cultism. The Church is ONE, just as the Lord is ONE! We seek fellowship with all believers, especially those of like-faith, even though we are constrained to take care lest we enter into error.

Fellowship with mainline, evangelical, Protestant ministries is encouraged. Sects that teach, encourage and practice strange things, *(et. al. Snake handlers; "that Jesus is not God";*

or that "the Holy Ghost is unnecessary for believers today," "Inclusionism," etc.) must be avoided. We are enjoined to *"have no fellowship with the unfruitful works of darkness...but rather reprove them."*

There will be those times when our Roman Catholic, Eastern Catholic, Methodist, Baptist, Lutheran, Presbyterian, and Episcopal brethren will extend their hand in fellowship. We encourage our bishops to join with them in establishing fellowship and, when possible, communion. Each Christian Faith Group must be viewed with a careful eye and it is expected that every bishop, prelate, cleric and deacon of this Church will look to their own Apostolic Offices for a sense of direction in those areas that may appear unclear.

This College does not enter into ecumenical worship services with Muslims, Buddhists, Hindus, or any other religion that

Relationships With Other Religious Bodies

we deem to be false and/or idolatrous. We may from time to time unite with the people of our communities, regardless of religious persuasion, for the purpose of social justice and community welfare. Having taken the foregoing position, let us further say that we do not subscribe to their gods nor do we give assent to their rituals, but we are never authorized to disrespect any man or woman of religion. We may disagree, *and disagree we must,* but we are enjoined to give every person the highest social regard accorded their office and person. We lose nothing by being polite and practicing tolerance of those who are religious people of goodwill.

This College discourages the use of any *Pentecostal* pulpit for political campaigns or as a candidate's platform. Please remember that we are the Church of the Lord Jesus Christ, the Kingdom of God in the earth. Our purpose for existence is to advertise our Sovereign, Jesus Christ, and Him only. If we allow ourselves to enter into the arena of political endorsements, we lose our effectiveness as *"Heralds of Holiness"* and endanger our *tax-exempt* status. We exist to serve the Lord in our nation as the 'moral consciences,' and to be the "Visible Presence of The Holy," ever warning mankind that *"righteousness exalts a nation, but sin is a reproach to any people."*

Chapter VII

LEVITICAL VESTMENTS and CODE OF DRESS

In 1970 we were consecrated in Boston, Massachusetts by the late Bishop Brumfield Johnson of the Mount Calvary Holy Church of America, Inc. Shortly thereafter, we returned to the denomination of our roots. And for a period of, *better than*, two decades we served the Church of God in Christ as Adjutant-Apostolic to the late Presiding Bishop James Oglethorpe Patterson, Sr. We coined the title *"Adjutant"* in the Pentecostal Community and formed the first Adjutants' Corps in the Church of God in Christ in September 1969. We were privileged to appoint, with the approval of the Presiding Bishop, *then*, Elders Phillip Aquilla Brooks, Roy L. H. Winbush, Floyd Eugene Perry, Beuford Terry, and Marcus L. Butler as the first Adjutants with us in the Church of God in Christ. Our first official assignment was to assist Bishop Patterson in the formal consecration of the newly appointed Bishop T. T. Scott of Northern Mississippi. We assisted the Fathers in making princes for the Lord's Church, and now we are privileged to assist and succeed some of those same princes in their ministries of apostleship.

The men of the *United Pentecostal Churches of Christ* (UPCC) asked us to sit with them and become their *Rabbi (Teacher)* or *Father-in-God* and that is what we have tried to do. But necessity was laid on us to assist brethren outside of ourselves as they sought to realign their communions with the Kingdom of God. It is our hope that this volume will begin to bring about the excellence in the Church that pleases God and glorifies Him in the earth.

The following article is intended to identify our proper *habit* within this distinct Kingdom system. This is the third version of the

Levitical Vestments and Code of Dress

original *"Dress Code"* that we were privileged to write for the Church of God in Christ in A.D., 1972. After forming the UPCC we employed the assistance of one of our sons who was priestly and who exhibited a desire to learn this ministry of servitude, Bishop *(Suffragan)* Eric Daniel Garnes of Brooklyn, New York. He created a re-write of our original text and assisted us in preparing this volume for this Discipline. This volume is the completion of several additional years of thought among us.

There will certainly be revisions in the days ahead but until then...this is the rule by which we should govern ourselves.

A Ministerial Dress Code is herein prepared so that we might effectively exemplify the beauty and dignity of holiness, showing ourselves an example to all believers in all things. This Code will prescribe and suggest Civil, Ceremonial *(Choir Dress)*, Liturgical, and

Academic Attire for the Bishops, Clergy and Diaconate of the Churches.

The effectiveness of this Code is contingent upon the commitment of every clerical member of the College to adhere to its standards at every level. By doing so we establish order, and a sincere acknowledgment of, and regard for spiritual authority.

<u>THE PRESIDING BISHOP</u>

As the apostle and primate of the Church, color and design distinctively and obviously separate the Presiding Bishop's garments from the rest of the offices named herein. The <u>principle</u> *color* of the Presiding Bishop's Office is SCARLET. It should be understood that the Presiding Bishop has the option of wearing *any* of the Church's liturgical colors *(ROMAN PURPLE, ENGLISH PURPLE or BLACK)*, when appropriate, but the use of the aforementioned color is to be reserved for the

Levitical Vestments and Code of Dress

Apostolic Office.

CHOIR DRESS

The Cassock is a close fitting garment, reaching the feet, and may be worn by all clergy as a symbol of the *servant*. The bishop wears this garment in deference to our Lord Jesus who instructed, *"they who would be chief among you, shall be servant of all."*

It should be noted that there are several types of Cassocks that are available to the Priesthood. *(1) There is the Choir Cassock, which is usually Anglican in Style and without Cincture since it is to be worn under other Vestments. (2) The Roman Cassock bears the simple coat-look with buttons beginning at the neck and continuing down the front of the garment to the floor. (3) The Soutain is the same as the Roman Cassock with the matching Manteletta (cape) attached at the shoulders. This Cassock is usually trimmed in the color of one's*

Office with matching Cincture. This particular Cassock is also called the "House Cassock" and is worn by bishops and priests within their daily offices or at occasional public or street functions. It is not a Worship Garment or a Celebration Vestment. On occasion, this garment may be worn at Conclaves or during "Magesterium" Sessions of the Church.

The Cincture is worn about the waist with the Cassock. It is the girdle and symbol of that with which our Lord *"girded Himself....with a towel to wash His disciple's feet."* This portion of the vestment is to be the same color as that of the Cassock with exception. The exception in this Church is when the Presiding Bishop raises one to Apostolic Chamberlain, Chaplain to the Presiding Bishop or Adjutant-Apostolic, all without episcopacy. In these cases the Presiding Bishop will grant the designated color and from the moment of the announcement,

Levitical Vestments and Code of Dress

the cleric so appointed may begin to wear the Cincture.

The Rochet is a ceremonial white linen or cotton garment, similar to the Surplice. The principle difference between this garment and the Surplice is that the length of the Surplice usually reaches the knees, while the Rochet reaches the floor. The sleeves of the Rochet differ from the Surplice in that the Rochet sleeve is made like unto a coat or a buffed-bell gathered at the wrist. This garment is the symbol of the Priesthood, which was given to Aaron and his sons, as well as those of us who draw nigh to the Altar of God to represent Christ to His people. It is the symbol of worship and only bishops or those who have Apostolic Dispensation to do so wear the Rochet.

The Chimere is the sleeveless outer-robe of the bishop. The symbol of this garment is that of the bishop's Prophetic Office in the

The Bishopric

Church as Chief Preacher and Defender of the Faith within his/her See. The specific color of this garment is SCARLET for the Presiding Bishop and Diocesan Bishops ONLY. There may be occasions when the Presiding Bishop might elect to wear ROMAN PURPLE with his brother-bishops or BLACK at a funeral or on a most solemn occasion. In any event, this garment is reserved for bishops who have been duly appointed and/or consecrated to that Office *by the laying on of the hands* by bishops who have Apostolic Succession and the Canonical Authority to do so.

The Stole or Tippet is the symbol of the *yoked one*. All clergy of the Church are authorized to wear this symbol, while the Presiding Bishop wears the Seal of the Church and of his/her Apostolic Office affixed thereunto. The Tippet is the symbol of Jurisdiction. It alone denotes the bishop's

Levitical Vestments and Code of Dress

territory or diocese when the Seals of his/her Office are affixed.

The Zucchetto is the bishop's Prayer Cap and must not be worn by any other than the bishop. The bishop ONLY wears a Zucchetto in Cassock, Soutain *(housedress)*, Choir Dress or Ceremonial Vestments. The Zucchetto is removed during Prayers of Invocation, the Consecration of the Host, Blessings, the Public Reading or Hearing of the Gospels of Jesus Christ and at the "All Hail" of Handel's Messiah. The bishop does not remove it, however, during the Prayer of Consecration at the ordination of elders and deacons or the Consecration of Bishops.

The Cross and Chain should be of precious gold or silver and may be worn by bishops ONLY. The Cross is the obvious message of the Church for the salvation of the world in Christ. The Cross may have a precious

The Bishopric

stone encrested in keeping with the bishop's desire. The chain from which it is suspended should be *(at least)* forty inches *(40")* in length (from end to end). The length will allow for proper wear with the civic attire.

The Episcopal Shoes/Slippers and Stockings for the Presiding Bishop shall be RED (Scarlet). There may be those times when the Presiding Bishop may select to wear the Black Buckled Slipper, but at no time shall any other episcopate, elder or cleric in the Church wear the Scarlet Slippers or any which resemble those of the Presiding Bishop's Office with any vestment. All other bishops may wear the ROMAN PURPLE stockings with their vestments ONLY. <u>At no time will purple stockings be worn with the Civic Attire. Black or off/black stockings, ONLY, will be worn with Civic Attire!!</u>

The Ring is the symbol of Royal Sonship

Levitical Vestments and Code of Dress

and episcopal collegiality. This Ring is usually signet or jeweled. It is worn on the right hand, ring finger. When it is worn, no other ring is proper except the Wedding Band for those bishops who are married. This same rule holds true when wearing the civic attire. We are never to wear ornamentation when in uniform. Loud buttons or carnations are completely out of order, regardless to the occasion, when in our vestments or civic attire.

Grooming Standards are vital if we are to maintain credibility among our people and in the world community. It is required that we wear our hair well cut and groomed at all times. Facial hair must be kept extremely well trimmed and always in proper and tasteful lengths. Manicures are encouraged. And since it is with our Hands that we impart Blessings, we encourage our bishops and clergy, alike, to take special care to attend to this matter. In the case of bishops, we would remind that *people venerate our Office by kissing our Episcopal Ring or our right Hand.* That alone should make us very careful about our public use and care of our hands.

Shoes must always be kept well heeled and shined. Stockings and/or socks must be worn in proper color and well groomed at all times.

Chapter VIII

CELEBRATION VESTMENTS

Celebration Vestments are usually worn when a specific service of worship requires the Celebration of the Lord's Broken Body and Shed Blood. When it is determined that Holy Communion will be served, and that there will be a Solemn Processional of the diaconate, clergy and episcopacy, the Presiding Bishop will adorn in CASSOCK, ROCHET or ALB, STOLE and CHASUBLE, with MITRE and CROSIER. In Celebration Vestments, it is not necessary for the Bishop to wear the Pectoral Cross, however, if the Cross is worn it should be suspended by the Cord of Red and Gold or solid Gold, for the Presiding Bishop, and Green and Gold for all other Ranks of the Bishopric who have received Apostolic Succession.

The Purple and Gold Cord can be used, however, this cord is used by Dispensation

The Bishopric

from the Presiding Bishop to subordinate prelates, from time to time.

The RED SLIPPERS and STOCKINGS are an optional wear in this garment and should be determined by the Presiding Bishop in consultation with his/her chief adjutant or chaplain.

Chapter IX

CIVIC WEAR (Bishops)

This is, perhaps, the simplest section to describe. The plain black suit or dress *(for clergywomen)* with the white clerical collar is the basic street dress for all clergy in the Church. Diaconate ordinariates will wear the *"Brother's Collar"* as their official civic attire.

Black shoes *(plain toe – heel-in)* and black stockings are the required accessories. At no time (in uniform) will earrings, necklaces, or excessive finger-rings be worn with this or any other Clerical Uniform.

Black Topcoats or overcoats *(plain)* are always tasteful, with a simple Black Hat for street-wear. We must avoid the use of gaudy, distracting items on our clothes, especially when in the uniform of our High and Holy Office.

The Bishopric

All clergy of the Church should wear the Black Breast Front with your uniform. However, in those cases where order dictates, bishops should wear their Roman Purple Breast Fronts while overseers may wear their English/Blue Purple Breast Fronts.

<u>The Pectoral Cross and Chain</u> *(of gold or silver)* is worn around the neck with the cross in the left breast pocket (over the heart) with the chain exposed. Overseers may wear the Silver Cross with the Scarlet Cord exposed over the breast in either the Black Breast Front or the Purple Breast Front. On occasion, the Presiding Bishop may elect to wear the Scarlet Breast Front with civic attire. But on any occasion, the Presiding Bishop's Dress is adorned with the Pectoral Cross and Episcopal Ring.

Chapter X

THE COLLEGE OF BISHOPS (Colors)

The Members of this College have the distinction of the same vestment as that of the Presiding Bishop with one reservation: *Bishops may not wear the Scarlet Slippers.*

The highest color of this Office is ROMAN (*Fuchsia*) PURPLE, with regard to the Cassock. Now since there are five ranks of the Bishopric recognized by our College, it is needful to make clear the color designation within each rank with regard to the Chimere, as follows:

The Presiding Bishop
SCARLET

The Ordinary *(Diocesan)*
SCARLET

The Coadjutor Bishop
SCARLET

The Suffragan Bishop
ROMAN PURPLE

The Bishopric

The Auxiliary Bishop
ROMAN PURPLE

The Overseer
BLACK

There may be times when bishops may elect to wear the BLUE PURPLE or BLACK Cassock or Chimere but during Collegial Conclaves *(meetings of the College of Bishops or settings when peers will be present)* all Joint College Bishops will adhere to the regimen set forth by the President Bishop.

The Civic Attire as described under the Presiding Bishop's Section is the same for all bishops with the exceptions described therein.

Chapter XI

OVERSEERS

These prelates are appointed, by the Presiding Bishops, upon the recommendation of the bishops in the dioceses. The basic cassock of this office is ENGLISH/BLUE PURPLE with matching Cincture. No other office within the College is permitted to wear this color *except* the Bishops and the Assistant Pastors at the NATIONAL CATHEDRAL of the United Pentecostal Churches of Christ in Cleveland, OH. *[Note: Other Presiding Bishops may also mandate the same for their Cathedral Center Assistants. When they do so, we will publish the same in the Annual Report.]*

All other items of Choir Dress are the same as described in the foregoing sections, with the following exception:

The Chimere worn by this office is always black and the Wrist Bands on the

Rochet are also Black.

Celebration Vestments

This Vestment is the same as that of any Celebrant at the Lord's Table *(as described in the foregoing Section)* with the exception of the use of a MITRE, ZUCHETTO *(skullcap)* or CROZIER.

Chapter XII

CIVIC WEAR (Overseers)

The Civic Wear of the Overseer and all other clergy is the same as that of a bishop with the following exceptions:

The Breast <u>Front</u> must be either BLACK or ENGLISH/BLUE PURPLE. The Cross should be silver, while the Suspension Cord must be Scarlet. The length should be between 36" and 40" from end to end. In the few instances where persons come to us as bishops from other Reformations without Apostolic Succession, the Presiding Bishops may authorize the continued use of the Gold Cross and Chain for this person who must use the rank of an overseer. Shoes and Stockings must be black *(stockings should be off black for ladies)*.

ALL OTHER DIRECTIVES APPLY.

Chapter XIII

ORDAINED and NON-ORDAINED CLERGY

The primary color of these offices shall be black and/or white. At no time shall these offices adorn themselves in any of the colors not authorized by the Church. Pastors may wear the Pulpit or Academic Gown for occasional Preaching Services as they deem fit. Such gown may bear the insignia of their Doctorate and the Velvet paneling, which is normal and proper to our usage. However, anything more than these are deemed inappropriate for use by our pastors and ordained preachers.

The Choir Dress for all ordained clergy is the same as that of the OVERSEER except the color of the Cassock shall be BLACK and without any trimming of color other than matching BLACK. And SURPLICES shall become the outer garment for Choir Dress.

Ordained and Non-Ordained Clergy

ADJUTANTS may have the distinctive cord of Roman Purple as issued by the chief adjutant, only at the recommendation of the Bishop of the said adjutant. Otherwise, the <u>Ceremonial and Choir Dress</u> of these offices is the same as that of any other elder.

Non-ordained ministers are restricted, in Ceremonial and Choir Dress, to the WHITE ALB.

Chapter XIV

DEACONS

Deacons are the chief servants of their pastors and as such, they have a distinctive Dress as *Servant-Ministers* within our Church. Their Civic Attire has been described as the same as that of all clergy within the Church except, they shall wear the Brothers Collar and the BLACK Breast at all times.

The WHITE ALB shall be the Ceremonial and Choir Dress of distinction for all deacons, while deacons who have received Ordination shall be granted the privilege of the Deacon's Stole of Coronation Tapestry.

It should be noted here that pastors may elect to have student ministers *(seminarians)* wear the Brothers Collar during their tenure as Candidates for Ordination. This is left entirely up to the pastors of the Churches. This might allow for some distinction, since non-ordained ministers cannot wear the full white collar until ordination. Be governed by your hearts and by the conduct of the student in question.

We trust that this brief overview of the Code of Dress for the clergy will answer questions and allow for us to *"walk by the same rule and mind the same things."* Each bishop is charged with the responsibility of insisting on the obedience of their people to these and all things that attend to our witness and message in this "end time."

Chapter XV

EPILOGUE

The question is often asked, *"What happens when a bishop or prelate dies?"* There have been those times when this question arises in families and this brief section is designed to offer some helpful hints in the event of the passing of the bishop, overseer or even the pastor of an assembly.

The first call, from the place of passing or transition, should be made to the Presiding Bishop of the Church. This allows him/her to interact with the family and the diocese or congregation from the very outset. The passing of a prelate or pastor is quite traumatic for the family and for the people over whom he/she presides. Contacting the Presiding Bishop offers an immediate sense of stability. *It is hoped that every bishop would make this provision available to their families so that the transition*

Epilogue

period and the memorial can be made easy for all concerned. Once the Presiding Bishop has been notified and has conferred with the nearest of kin, the Presiding Bishop then appoints the chief adjutant of the Church to enter the area to act as his/her Apostolic Emissary. The chief adjutant superintends the final arrangements in cooperation with the family and in keeping with the Reformation's traditions.

A Memorial Service is held when there are no remains present for the said Service. A Funeral or Homegoing Liturgy is held when the remains are present and on a bier in full view of the worshippers and mourners.

Families are encouraged to practice modesty in the matter of funeral expenses. Families must live long after the prelate or pastor is gone. In the place of floral tributes, families can establish a scholarship fund in the

The Bishopric

deceased leader's name or some other worthy charitable project that was dear to the deceased leader's heart.

Whenever possible, the Presiding Bishop's Honor Guard, *"The Order of the Apostolic Knights of Pentecost (OAK of P),"* can serve as the Guard and/or Pallbearers for the funeral of a bishop or overseer. In the case of the Presiding Bishop, the National Corps of Adjutants shall serve as the Pallbearers, while the OAK of P maintains the Vigil Watch.

The final burial vestment of the bishop should be, either, the highest Celebration Dress or Choir Dress. This depends on what the Presiding Bishop and College of Bishops will wear for the funeral. *If the celebration garment is selected, the funeral director should be notified so that the casket can accommodate the bishop's miter without intrusion.* No Episcopal Ring or Pectoral Cross shall be buried with the

Epilogue

bishop. The Pastoral Staff shall not be buried with the bishop. A "<u>Chronicle or Certificate of Ministry, Episcopacy and Death</u>" should be placed in the casket with the deceased but <u>no other</u> precious sacramental items may be buried with the bishop.

In those cases where the spouse of the pastor of the assembly is in ministry and in possession of Holy Orders, the bishop having jurisdiction should look to see if the surviving spouse can be appointed as successor. If so, the bishop should make the appointment as soon as possible after the burial of the bishop. Even if the appointment is *interim* it will give some sense of continuance and stability during that time of transition. If, in the event, the spouse is not a minister but has been known to work closely with the deceased pastor or leader, it would be wise for the bishop to allow the spouse's opinions to weigh heavily on his/her

The Bishopric

decision regarding a successor.

It is also hoped that our bishops and pastors will write their wishes and forward sealed envelopes to their Presiding Bishop addressed as follows: *"TO BE OPENED IN THE EVENT OF MY DEATH."* The instructions therein will be of tremendous value as the successor-bishop works to fill the void.

Congregations are enjoined to establish policies and or trusts that will care for the surviving spouse in the event of the loss of their pastor. No congregation can take care of <u>two First Ladies or First Families</u>! Your church will need to compensate your new pastor and it is needful for every congregation of your Reformation to be wise and prepare.

Pastors should speak to another pastor about their desires. This will help the surviving family when the time comes to articulate the desires of the predecessor. Families have a way

Epilogue

of becoming "unbelievable" when the head of the family dies. People look for a reason to hold them in disbelief and your care to articulate your desires and vision will stem a lifetime of bitterness and pain.

We have attempted to place the bulk of our thoughts in this brief volume and constitution for the College of Bishops. This treaty is designed to lend some assistance to those bishops and prelates who serve the Lord in this lonely office. Many look at this seat and lust for it. But to ascend to this chair one should know that they have reached the foot of Mount Calvary and the climb is for the rest of your solitary life. This office has its time of glory and is filled with love and the adoration of the people. But when the *Palm Sundays* have ended and the third day before *Easter* comes, all too quickly we experience the brunt of the cruel crowd and the sharp blade of steel which pierces our heart when the people we serve cry, *"CRUCIFY HIM!"*

- - - - - - - - - - - -

APPENDIX

The Historical Document on Apostolic Succession
as transferred to
The United Pentecostal
Churches of Christ

By The Grace of Almighty God, and with an Eye, single to His Glory, I,

~ JESSE DELANO ELLIS, II ~

A bishop in our Lord's Church,

Do publicly proclaim and defend our right as one of the legitimate Successors to Christ and the Apostles on any occasion of the Consecration and Ordination of a brother in Christ and son in the Episcopacy. We Consecrate and grant Apostolic Succession to:

(Name of the Candidate Bishop)

and to present him to the Flock of God as a Prince in our Lord's Church. We therefore offer this apology as our right and warrant to do this thing in the congregation of the Saints.

The Bishopric

On the fourth day of September, in the year of our Lord, One thousand, Nine hundred, Sixty four, Anno Domini (A.D.), we received Holy Orders from His Grace, The Most Reverend Ozro Thurston Jones, I, *Senior Bishop* of the Church of God in Christ at Philadelphia, Pennsylvania in the United States of America. Having served the Lord's Church as an Ordained Priest (Elder), we were selected for Episcopal Office and Consecrated to the same by The Most Reverend Brumfield Johnson, Senior Bishop and Establishmentarian of the Mount Calvary Holy Church of America, Incorporated at Boston (Dorchester), Massachusetts on the Eleventh day of January in the Year of our Lord, One-thousand, Nine-hundred, Seventy, Anno Domini during the Mid-Winter Convention of that Church. The Board of Bishops of Mount Calvary assisted Bishop Johnson in the Ordination.

Document on Historical Apostolic Succession

We were affirmed in that office by The Most Reverend William David Charles Williams, *Senior Bishop* of the Church of God in Christ, (International) on the Seventeenth day of April, in the year of our Lord, One thousand, Nine hundred, Seventy, Anno Domini, at New York City in the United States. His Grace was assisted by The Right Reverend Carl Edward Williams, and The Right Reverend Reuben Timothy Jones, both, *Ordinaries* of the same Communion. Bishops Williams and Jones were themselves possessors of Holy Orders from the Methodist Episcopal Church in the United States.

Bishop Reuben Timothy Jones had been ordained by Bishop Frederick Pierce Corson, *President of the World Methodist Conference and Prelate of the Pennsylvania-Delaware Conference of the Methodist Episcopal Church*, on the Twenty-fourth day of December, in the year of our Lord, One thousand, Nine hundred, Forty six, Anno Domini.

Hereinafter is the Historical Connection:

The Methodist Episcopal Church was descendant from the Church of England ("Anglicana" = Anglican). The same Methodist Church was formed by The Reverend Father John Wesley, who, was a possessor of Holy Orders from the Church of England. Father John Wesley's Apostolic Succession was received through the unbroken Stream that was brought to England through the Roman Catholic Church. One, Saint Augustine of Rome, Italy, brought, from the Holy See, the message of Christ to the English (Saxons) in the Fifth Century, A.D.

The Church at Rome received her Patriarchy from the Church at Ephesus. The Church at Ephesus received her Patriarchy from the Church at Antioch. The Church at

Document on Historical Apostolic Succession

Antioch received her Patriarchy from the Church at Jerusalem. It was at Jerusalem where the Church was formed and born of the Holy Ghost. It was also at Jerusalem where our Lord's appointed Apostles governed Christ's Church and appointed bishops as their successors. As each Patriarchy fell and the Church was dispersed through persecution, Rome received the guardianship of the Church until Augustine was sent to the Normans and the Saxons and the Church of England was ultimately formed. The Stream of Apostolic Succession remained unbroken through Wesley, Asbury and two hundred years later, to Corson, Jones, Williams, and then to me.

The foregoing chronicle summarizes the Apostolic Succession we have received and impart from the "Western Stream" of this historical and glorious Succession. Therefore, the Church of the Western Heritage is traced

The Bishopric

from Christ and His Apostles unto us in this Twenty-first Century. Any bishop or elder that we shall elevate, or that shall be elevated by any bishop whom we have elevated will be in the Stream, which will make him/her a successor to Christ and the Apostles as well.

As Primus Episcopos *(Presiding Bishop)* of the United Pentecostal Churches of Christ, we may be called to serve as Principal Consecrator for servants of Christ who have received election or appointment to Episcopacy. Should we accept the charge to do so we also bring to these sons of God, Apostolic Succession from the "Eastern Stream" of the ancient pilgrim Church. Any bishop that we shall ordain and consecrate shall have dual claim to Apostolic Succession as shown in the chronicle as follows:

Jesus Christ, the Messiah; *[hereinafter all dates refer to A.D. or Anno Domini]* 33-37,

Document on Historical Apostolic Succession

Apostle Thomas; 33, Apostle Bartholomew; 33-45, Apostle Thaddeus; 45-81, Haggai *(one of the Seventy commissioned by Jesus in the Gospel of Luke 10:1)*; 48-81, Mari; 90-107, Abris *(a relative of our Lord Jesus' mother, Mary)*; 130-152, Oraham,1 [Abraham] (a citizen of Kashkar, Western China); 171-190, Yacob,1 [Jacob] (a relative of Joseph the Carpenter, our Lord Jesus' stepfather); 191-203, Ebed M'Shikha; 205-220, Akhu D'Awu; 224-244, Shakhlupa; 247-326, Papa Bar Gaggai (the first to hold the title "Catholicos [meaning = 'holder of all'], who moved the "See" to Baghdad, just fifty miles north of ancient Babylon); 328-341, Shimun Bar Sabbai [Simeon or Simon]; 345-347, Shahdost; 350-358, Bar Bashmin; 383-393, Qaiyuma; 399-411, Eskhag [Isaac] (this Patriarch caused the Church to flourish in Iran and during his reign, much of the persecutions ceased. During his tenure, the Council Nicea was formed and from that the "Nicene Creed" was given to the Church); 411-415, Akhi; 415-420, Yoalaha, 1 [Babu]; 484-496, Agag [Acacius]; 496-502, Bawa, 11 [Babowi] (this Bishop assumed the title "Patriarch of the East" in A.D. 498, and the title is still used today); 505-523, Sheela; 524-535, Narsai*; 424-538, Elisha*; (this represents a time of duel Patriarchate); 539-540, Polos [Paul]; 552-567, Yosip [Joseph]; 570-581, Khazqiyil [Ezekiel]; 581-595, Arzunaya Eshuyow, 1; 596-604, Garmagaya Sorishu, 1; 605-608, Partaya Greghor [Gregory]; 628-644, Gdalaya Eshuyow,11 (an Arab who sent the first known Missionary to Peking, China in 635, A.D.); 647-650, Kdayawa Eshuyow, 111; 681-684, Gewargis, 1 [George]; 684-692, Bar Marta Yokhannan, 11; 714-728, Sliwazkah; 731-740, Peythyon; 741-741, Awa (Awa translated the Old Testament into Syriac from Greek for scholarly use and only served one year); 752-754, Surin; 754-773, Yacob, 1; 774-778, Khnanishu, 11; 780-820, Timotheus, 1 [Timothy] (In 781, A.D., a monument was erected in China to commemorate one hundred, fifty years of Christianity in that country. The erectors stated that Khnanishu, 1, was Patriarch at that time. The monument shows the cross above the clouds and lotus blossoms, signifying its superiority over Islam and Bhuddism.); 820-824, Eshu Bar Non [Joshua, Son of Nun]; 825-832, Gewargis, 11; 832-836, Soreshu, 11; 837-850, Margaya Oraham, 11; 850-852, Teadasis [Theodosius]; 860-872, Suwaya Sargia; 873-884, Garmay Annush D'Beth; 884-892, Bar Narsai Yokhannan, 111; 892-898, Yokhannan, 1V; 900-905, Bar Ogare Yokhannan, 1; 906-937, Abraza Oraham, 111; 937-949, Ammanoel,11 [Emmanuel]; 961-962, Karkhaya Esrail [Israel]; 963-986, Garmagaya

The Bishopric

Odishu (servant of Jesus); 967-1000, Aari Aturaya; 1001-1012, Yokhannan, Vl; 1013-1022, Bar Nazuk Yokhannan, V11; 1028-1049, Terhan Elia, 1; 1049-1057, Bar Tragala Yokhannan, V111; 1057-1072, Bar Zanbur Soreshu, 111; 1072-1090, Bar Ars Aturaya Odishu, 11; 1092-1109, Bar Shlemon Makkikha, 1; [son of Solomon]; 1111-1132, Bar Magli Elia, 11; 1133-1135, Bar Soma; 1135-1136, Bar Gabbara; 1138-1147, Odishu,111; 1148-1175, Esuyow, V11; 1176-1190, Abukhalim Elia, 111; 1191-1222, Bar Qaiyuma Yoalaha, 11; 1222-1226, Sorishu, 1V; 1226-111256, Sorishu, V; 1257-12265, Makkikha, 11 (this Patriarch moved the Patriarchy to Iraq); 1265-1281, Epiphanius Dinkha, 1; 1281-1318, Bar Turkaye Yoalaha, 111 [son of the Turks]; 1318-1328, Arbilaya Timotheus, 11 (With Timothy of Arabela, a hereditary Patriarchy began. This Office was passed from 'uncle' to 'nephew', and continued until 1976 when the present 'Catholicos' was elected by the Episcopal College); 1329-1359, Dinkha, 11; 1359-1368, Dinkha, 111; 1369-1392, Shimun, 111 (during this period, the Mongol rejected Christianity and launched a purge in Turkey which began the extermination of the Eastern Church. The Church at its peak was better than eighty four million souls strong, but was reduced to less than two million in the purge); 1403-1407, Shimun, V1; 1491-1504, Elia, V; 1507-1538, Shimun,V11 (from this point until 1976, all Patriarchs of the Church of the East were named "Shimun" [Simon], generally with another name proceeding, with the number referring to the generation of "Shimun"); 1538-1551, Shimun, V111 (during this period the Patriarchy moved to the Azerbaijan province of northwestern Iran. Following this, the Church of the East moved to Turkish Kurdistan.

The Bishopric

Persecution nearly destroyed the Eastern Church even to the present time. The See was moved to the United States during World War 1 (It is now back in Baghdad); 1552- 1558, Dinkha Shimun, 1X (it is here that the Roman doctrines were introduced into the Eastern Church. Deep and enduring divisions entered into the Church of the East, which had been weakened by persecutions. Roman, Byzantine, Jacobite, and Armenian sources were sought after Tamerlane's massacre, which contributed to the multiplicity of separate Eastern Churches having a common history back to the Apostles); 1558-1580, Yolaha Shimun, X; 1680-1600, Dinkha Shimun, X1; 1600-1653, Elia Shimun, X11; 1653-1690, Eshuyow Shimun, X111; 1690-1692, Yoalaha Shimun, X1V; 1692-1700, Dinkha Shimun, XV; 1700-1740, Shlemon Shimun, XV1; 1740-1741, Mikhail Shimun, XV11; 1741-1820, Yonan Shimun,

Document on Historical Apostolic Succession

XV111; 1820-1860, Oraham Shimun, X1X; 1860-1903, Ruwil [Reuben] Shimun,XX.

Ruwil Shimun, XX, consecrated Mar Abdisho Antonius, Metropolitan of the Syro-Chaldean Christians of Malabar, India, on the Seventeenth day of December, in the year of our Lord, One thousand, Eight hundred, Sixty two. On the Twenty fourth day of July, in the year of our Lord, One thousand, Eight hundred, Ninety nine, he consecrated Mar Baasilius, Metropolitan of India. On the Thirtieth day of November, in the year of our Lord, One thousand, Nine hundred and Two, he also consecrated Mar Jacobus [U. Vernon Herford], Bishop of Mercia and Middlesex, in an attempt to extend the influence of the Eastern Church.

1903-1918, Binyamin [Benjamin] Shimun, XX1; 1918-1920, Polos [Paul] Shimun, XX11; 1920-1975, Eshai Shimun, XX111. Eshai Shimun has the Office of Catholicos-

The Bishopric

Patriarch thrust upon him at the age of twelve, upon the murder of his uncle, Polos Shimun. To escape Turkish persecutions, he moved his See to San Francisco, California in the United States. In the year of our Lord, One thousand, Nine hundred, and Seventy three he abdicated the See and was assassinated two years later.

Following the death of Eshai Shimun, the See was vacant for several years. Rival Patriarchs were elected. The hereditary Patriarchate was ended and the See returned to Baghdad. Negotiations between rival parties are continuing to determine the true successor.

On the Twenty-eighth day of February, in the year of our Lord, One thousand, Nine hundred, Twenty five, Mar Jacobus consecrated Paulos [William Stanley McBean Knight], Bishop of Kent. On the Thirtieth day of October, in the year of our Lord, One thousand, Nine hundred, Thirty one, Mar Paulos consecrated

Mar Georgius [Hugh George deWillmott Newman], Assistant Bishop of the See of Kent. On the Thirteenth day of April, in the year of our Lord, One thousand, Nine hundred, Fifty two, Mar Georgius consecrated Mar Charles D. Boltwood, Archbishop of England.

On the Third of May, in the year of our Lord, One thousand, Nine hundred, Fifty nine, Archbishop Boltwood consecrated Mar Yokhannan [John Marion Stanley], Bishop of Washington State in the United States of America, later elevated to Archbishop Metropolitan of the Syro-Chaldean Archdiocese of North America. Archbishop Stanley received Mar Jacobus [James Andrew Gaines] into the Church of the East on the Fifth of March, in the year of our Lord, One thousand, Nine hundred, Sixty nine. Bishop Gaines had been consecrated in the Line of the Russian and Ukrainian Orthodox Churches. Archbishop

The Bishopric

Stanley elevated Bishop Gaines to Archbishop Metropolitan of the Autocephalous Syro-Chaldean Archdiocese of the Eastern United States of America.

On the Thirty-first of October, in the year of our Lord, One thousand, Nine hundred, Seventy six, Mar Jacobus [Archbishop Gaines], assisted by Mar Yokhannan [Archbishop Stanley], consecrated Mar Uzziah Bar Evyon [Bertram S. Schlossberg], Bishop of the Northeastern Diocese of the United States of America. Co-Consecrators were Archbishop Andrew Praaxky and Bishop Anthony Praxky, both of the Slaaavic Orthodox Church. Mar Uzziah [Bishop Schlossberg] was elevated to Archbishop Metropolitan of the Syro-Chaldean Church of North America, now known as the Evangelical Apostolic Church of North America. This elevation was granted by Mar Jacobus [Archbishop Gaines] on the Tenth day of

Document on Historical Apostolic Succession

September, in the year of our Lord, One thousand, Nine hundred, Seventy eight on the occasion of Archbishop Gaines' retirement.

In the year of our Lord, One thousand, Nine hundred, Ninety five, the Evangelical Apostolic Church of North America entered into collegial fellowship with the Anglican-Apostolic Communion of Believers called the United Pentecostal Churches of Christ. Archbishop Schlossberg, who resides in Jerusalem, Israel, sent Bishop Robert Woodward Burgess, II, a descendant of the "Eastern *(Church)* Stream," who, having received consecration from the hands of Archbishop Schlossberg, to the Holy Convocation of the United Pentecostal Churches of Christ. His Grace was mandated to assist us in the consecration of our Second College of Bishops and to impart to each of our sons that coveted Apostolic Succession from the Eastern Stream, while we imparted the

The Bishopric

same Succession from the Western Stream.

Bishop Schlossberg did also pass that same Eastern Succession on to us in moments of private devotions and thus we, impart this same Apostolic Blessing on to worthy Servants of Christ. Indeed we are one with the Apostles and Patriarchs who have passed on into the heavens. We are one with the entire Body of Christ, but that which assures us best is the personal baptism of the Holy Ghost, Who lives and abides within believers forever. Our conduct recaptures all of those things that best resemble the ancient pilgrim Church, while holding fast to that form of doctrine which we have heard and have been taught. We do not contend for Apostolic Succession as though it were the only means whereby legitimate leadership for the Church may be had. Neither do we believe that Apostolic Succession avails anything in the matter of salvation. We do,

Document on Historical Apostolic Succession

however, use this means to herald the privilege of the unbroken chain of Historical Succession for those who possess this treasure. We would also encourage our Pentecostal Brethren to appreciate and understand the historical significance attached to this part of our Apostolic History.

We issue this Defense by the Grace of Almighty God, this day, in this year of our Lord, Anno Domini, in the United States of America.

Prepared and Defended by us in this Thirty-third Anniversary Year of our Consecration to the Episcopacy, in the Name of Our Lord Jesus.

+ J. Delano Ellis, II, D.D.
Presiding Bishop, United Pentecostal Churches of Christ, and President, The Joint College of African-American Pentecostal Bishops

January 2003, A.D.

BIBLIOGRAPHY

Principle Sources for the Line of Succession:

Aprem, Mar. *Chaldean-Syrian Church in India.* Kerala, India: Mar Narsai Press, 1977.

McBirnie, William. S. *The Search for the Twelve Apostles.* Wheaton, Illinois: Tyndale House Publishers, 1973.

Ellis, II, Jesse. D. *Apostolic Succession in the United Pentecostal Churches of Christ.* Cleveland, Ohio: PCC Publishers, 1993.

Odishu, Mar. *The Marganitha (The Pearl).* Kerala, India: Mar Timotheus Memorial Publishers, 1965.

And other Minutes and Journals of Episcopates and Christian Reformations.

ISBN 1553958489
9 781553 958482

Printed in Great Britain
by Amazon.co.uk, Ltd.,
Marston Gate.